ACT ACCORDINGLY
A PHILOSOPHICAL FRAMEWORK

COLIN WRIGHT

Asymmetrical Press
Missoula, Montana

Published by Asymmetrical Press, Missoula, Montana.

Library of Congress Cataloging-In-Publication Data
Act accordingly / Colin Wright — 1st ed.
ISBN: 978-1-938793-17-2
eISBN: 978-1-938793-16-5
WC: 10,107
1. Self-Help. 2. Philosophy. 3. How To.
4. Inspiration. 5. Awesome.

Cover design by Colin Wright
Formatted in beautiful Montana
Printed in the U.S.A.
Typeset in Garamond

Publisher info:
Website: www.asymmetrical.co
Email: howdy@asymmetrical.co
Twitter: @asympress

For all the people with massive potential
but little idea how to use it.

Act Accordingly

CONTENTS

1. YOU ONLY LIVE ONCE

YOU HAVE EXACTLY ONE LIFE in which to do everything you will ever do. Act accordingly.

This is a wonderful and versatile concept to live by. Not only does it put the focus on the fact that you only live once, and therefore should make decisions based on the span of time you have available (which will be different based on who you are and the life you live), but it also makes no assertions as to what decisions you should make based on that information.

For some people, 'act accordingly' will mean jumping out of planes. For others, it will mean reading the complete works of Shakespeare. For others still, it will mean writing their own works, or playing a lot of Tetris, or eating pie. All of the pie.

This philosophy has been immensely liberating for me, because it helps me refocus on what's really important at any given moment, in any situation.

If I'm trying to decide whether or not to take on a new client, I think about how many years I might have left and calculate whether the time traded for the money offered would be worth it. Would the payoff be worth the time given up? Would my overall happiness increase or decrease as a result? And would it bring me closer to my goals? Is there another way to get closer to those goals that doesn't involve taking on this client? Would the project involve personal suffering, and if so, would it be worth bearing for the reward?

Far more than just a phrase, acting accordingly is a framework for decision-making that places importance where it belongs: on you and how you spend your time within the context of your life.

2. FREEDOM AS A FOCUS

I SPEND A WHOLE LOT of time trying to increase my level of freedom.

I don't mean 'increase my freedom' as a political statement, nor as a religious or philosophical one. It means having more options to choose from in all aspects of my life.

In practice, this means you choose your path — your beliefs, your relationships, your work — in part based on how many options are provided or taken away. All else being equal, a job that would give you greater flexibility in terms of promotion would be better than the alternative, and the same goes for a philosophy. A set of beliefs and personal rules that allow for a great deal of evolution and growth are superior to ones that do not.

Even so, most people find themselves pulled toward strict philosophies with black and white responses to questions that require greyscale answers.

The popularity of these philosophies can be partially attributed to this 'Yes or No' approach to answering very complicated questions. After all, who sounds more certain and confident: a person who answers your questions with absolute certainty, or someone who asks you a question in return?

Although the former may have a faster, more certain-sounding answer, it's the latter person — asking his or her question — who is more likely to eventually provide an answer with subtlety and precision. The concept of 'one size fits all' may be great when it comes to socks, but it's a sad practice indeed when it comes to personal philosophies that shape the way we live our lives.

So if black and white isn't the way to go, what is?

To answer that question, let me ask you a question. Which is better: to have nice pots, pans, spatulas, and knives, or to be a skilled chef?

This isn't a trick question, and there isn't a hard and fast answer that will always be the right one. But in most cases, being an experienced chef is the superior option over simply having high-end cooking equipment.

A chef is a person who can take any cooking tools and wield them confidently. Chefs can turn raw materials — even those of dubious quality — into something edible, and more than likely something that's also a pleasure to eat. They're versatile. They can learn new tricks along the way and adjust their styles over time.

They are, above all else, capable when it comes to food. That capability is what makes the difference, not the tools they use. The right tools in the wrong hands are less valuable than the wrong tools in the right hands.

Capability is just as important when developing your philosophical framework. Not in exactly the same way — very seldom are philosophical debates settled with a cook-off — but because capability allows for immense versatility and malleability; two traits that are vital if you're going to have a rugged, all-purpose, ever-evolving philosophy.

I mentioned before that freedom is the focus of my time. If I'm going to be capable of adjusting my trajectory as time goes by, I'll need to have a core that is as flexible and resilient as that goal. Something adaptable that will allow me to learn new things and make decisions based on the best available information.

If you're able to build such a structure — one that bends in the wind, rather than stubbornly breaking — you can fill it with simple concepts that then become magnetic north for your moral compass.

For me, 'act accordingly' is a mantra of sorts. Doing so allows me to be in constant flux, but still strive for the best decision-making in a given situation. Whether I'm reminding myself of how little time I have to make use of, or something more specific — this pie is delicious and you're hungry, act accordingly — it gives me permission to move forward while choosing the best path contextually, rather than based on preexisting rules that may or may not apply to my current situation.

To me, the best rules increase my level of freedom, rather than fence me in. They guide, rather than conceal. They add value, rather than take it away.

That's what it means to roll with the punches. That's what it means to act accordingly.

3. IT'S NOT ABOUT BEING SELFISH

IT'S EASY TO LOOK AT someone who's redefining their life, perhaps taking more time for themselves and their hobbies and the kind of work they've always wanted to do, and say, 'Wow, when did they become so selfish? Why are they trying so hard to dodge their responsibilities and to avoid paying their dues like the rest of us?'

Becoming a better version of yourself is not about selfishness or laziness. It's about optimization and self-improvement and taking the time to figure out what is best for you and those around you. It may mean doing a complete 180 in terms of priorities and where you expend your effort. It may mean skipping steps and dodging the usual hurdles that you, yourself, or life throws in your way.

Those who would look upon such actions as lazy are not taking in the big picture and are failing to realize that it's not purposeless labor that makes someone productive or respectable. It's the result of that labor and the value it brings to others.

Is it noble to work 100 hours a week to accomplish what could be done in 40? Is it virtuous to spend 40 hours on a project that could be delivered in 10? Certainly not, yet for some reason we treat 'hard work' as if it's an end unto itself, rather than a means to an end. We should respect the value added, not the effort exerted. An ox in the field can plow a certain amount of acreage, but a human with a post-industrial machine can do 100 times as much in a quarter of the time. This should be celebrated, and so should redefining oneself to be more productive.

Of course, you have to make sure that as you redefine yourself and your lifestyle that you aren't falling into bad habits along the way. It's incredibly easy to get caught up in the journey and lose sight of the goals, so it's important to not only stay on track, but to reevaluate that track from time to time to make sure you're still on the right one.

It may be that the shortest distance between you and your ideal lifestyle is halfway down one path, a third of the way down another, a tenth of the way down another, and so forth.

It's also common to see people switching up their lives, only to fall into another habit-prison a few months later, the only difference being that the new one is made up of different materials. Maybe you were caught up in earning money as an end rather than a means to an end, and you replace that path with extreme philosophical dogma of one sort or another.

Ideally, your path will grant you new, purpose-driven momentum. Everything you do should be purpose-driven, because that means you're choosing each step intentionally. You're not just slogging around — you're doing something at all times. Even if it's drinking a glass of orange juice or walking the dog, you know why you're doing these things. Your every move needn't be a revelatory moment or statement in order for it to be purposeful.

I've found that maintaining this purpose-driven lifestyle requires near-constant experimentation, because otherwise, how can you know your purpose is the right one for who you are at this very moment?

There's much ado about 'the meaning of life,' which is silly, because that purpose — the pursuit of which is your meaning — changes day by day, hour by hour, minute by minute. Yes, I know, biologically the meaning of life is to reproduce and pass on our genes, but intellectually we often need more than that. We're ever-moving toward some goal or another, and most people flutter around in so many different directions at all times that it's no wonder they seldom make it very close to realizing the fulfillment of their purpose.

Hone in on what's consequential to you — what's more important to you than anything else — and then move in its direction like iron to a magnet. This is the thing that's more important to you than anything else; what could possibly be more critical than moving toward it? Working another double-shift at the job in which you find no fulfillment so you can afford the down payment on another social symbol you'll use or wear once before burying it in a closet?

Identify that goal and set it in your mind. Visualizing won't bring you any closer to it, but it will help you do what needs to be done in order to get there.

I know your ideal lifestyle seems far away. Many important things are somewhat pie-in-the-sky dreams. But these dreams are achievable, you just have to get moving early and throw a lot of time and energy into them. If it was easy, everyone would accomplish all of their dreams all the time and books like this wouldn't be necessary. Unfortunately, that's not the case, but you can be the exception.

Redefining yourself — and your dreams — is not about being lazy. It's about being a bullet of intention flying toward a vitally important target. Consider that there might not be a later. Consider that today might be your last chance to make headway on that goal. Consider how you'll feel when you're close to achieving your goal. And how you'll feel once you've achieved it. Act accordingly.

4. LET'S FAIL UNTIL WE DON'T

CHALLENGES SHOULD BE A FREQUENT and welcome part of any person's life.

Unfortunately, many of us do everything we can to avoid challenges — to make life a little bit easier here, a little less stressful there — so that by the time we reach our 20s and 30s, a lot of life's frictions have been sanded down to a slippery finish.

What we often fail to realize when doing the sanding is that it's the friction we're eliminating that gives us proper grip to reach our next destination. Without challenges — and without the drudgery and despair and pain and exertion that come with them — we are doomed to stay more or less the same as we are today. Even when we kick a whole lot of ass, we should always be moving forward, toward an even more ass-kicking version of ourselves.

Of course, it's easier to theorize about challenges being useful than actually going out and finding, facing, and overcoming them. Most of us have been hardwired from a very young age to approach challenges only with a great sense of fear and overwhelm. If we don't do well on our upcoming test, we're doomed to a lifetime of working in fast food. If we don't nail the interview, we'll probably be poor our entire lives.

For most of us, life is one monumental undertaking after another. Each endeavor is so pregnant with possibility and the potential for failure; it's no wonder we're hesitant to take up the reins on another, even if it may help us out down the line. Stable ground and maintaining the status quo start to look pretty damn good after a dozen or so years of pre-real-life in academia, followed by any amount of time as a wage slave.

The thing to realize is that throughout our pasts, it hasn't been the challenges that scared us, but the failures. The idea that we may reach new heights is heartening, but the chance that we may stumble, fall, and hit every branch on the way down is paralyzing.

Often, challenges that come loaded with the

promise of great reward if we perform also hold potential doom should we botch. As such, a deep-seated fear of failure is the souvenir most of us end up taking home from school, work, and any other challenges we face from a very young age.

And there's nothing wrong with having a healthy respect for failure. One shouldn't aim to fail any more than one should be proud of it, but we also shouldn't be afraid of the occasional blunder. Settling makes for an exceedingly easy life, certainly, but not one that anyone would envy. It's a default lifestyle. A vanilla fate.

Far better to acknowledge failure for what it is: a step along the way to success.

So long as you're willing to pick yourself up after a loss and get back in the race, there's nothing that can stop you from winning eventually. If you want something badly enough, the only person who could stand in the way of your someday success is you.

It's not the most inspiring call to arms, I know. 'Let's fail until we don't!' But it's true. It's also reliable. It means you can achieve anything in the world, so long as you're willing to stubbornly stick with it and ignore the ego-bruises you'll take along the way. It means that you can learn while you work toward success and may even change your definition of what it means to win. That's okay — learning that the path you're on is the wrong one is certainly a victory, so long as you act on that information.

Ask any successful person you know and they'll tell you the same thing. Champions-from-birth are few and far between. Each and every person at the top of his or her field has a résumé littered with 'almosts' and accidents. Every gold medalist has been an also-ran; every tycoon has made the wrong deals.

What distinguishes these people is that they didn't stop. They didn't lose the first big race of their career and then hang up their running shoes. They didn't bet on the wrong pony and then get a job as a janitor (unless they were pushing the mop to earn enough money to start investing again).

Living life to the fullest is not about winning every time and avoiding the aspects of life that prove too onerous. It's about unabashedly facing challenges, failures, and yes, even successes with a smile, moving ever-forward toward a more ideal lifestyle and a better version of yourself.

5. ON CONFIDENCE

CONFIDENCE MEANS KNOWING THE VALUE of your knowledge, while maintaining awareness of how much you have left to learn.

A confident person knows enough to know how much she doesn't know. This allows her to be humble without staring at the floor, and to ask questions without worrying about looking ignorant. She knows that ignorance is a temporary affliction remedied only by asking the right questions.

Because knowledge will allow her to get where she needs to go and help her become who she wishes to be, a confident person values it above most other things. Knowledge isn't flashy, but there are no bounds to what one can achieve with it.

Confidence is being willing to defend your beliefs, or change them, based on new information.

A person without beliefs is like a ship with no mast or oars, and someone who is unwilling to change her beliefs when new information becomes available is just as lost.

There's a perceived honor in 'staying the course' even as time moves forward and facts evolve. But this honor is illusory. What on earth could be good about someone who is unwilling to change her mind when the world around her has shifted? To call such a person honorable would be like calling a time-traveling peasant from the Bronze Age honorable for maintaining that the Earth is flat, even as he views its roundness from space. Or celebrating a technology CEO who runs his business into the ground by stubbornly investing all his money in fax machines and pagers, even as those technologies drift into obscurity.

That's not honor. It's a stubborn refusal to admit to having ever been wrong. A confident person doesn't fear having been wrong: she's just happy to be more right now than she was before.

Confidence is sharing what you have to offer without apology, while also accepting what others have to offer.

There's a predisposition among many proud individuals to accept as little help from others as possible because they fear it might lead to a perception of their being weak. There's little good to be said of those who live off others, certainly, but to refuse help when it's necessary (or even just beneficial) is not the same as confidence.

A confident person is happy to accept a hand up when she needs it, and to offer the same to others. Confidence allows a person to focus on others outside of herself because she needs no additional glory — she feels pretty darn good already. If she can help others feel the same by accepting their help or offering her own, all the better.

Confidence is understanding both you and someone else can be right, despite holding different opinions.

There's a common misperception that in order to be confident, one must be in the right most of the time. Confident people must be so because they hold superior opinions and beliefs, right? They probably have greater stockpiles of knowledge. They probably come from more educated backgrounds.

This couldn't be further from the truth. While learning all you can from as many sources as possible certainly helps, simply knowing a lot of facts doesn't make a person any more right than her peers. Most opinions, in fact, are held from a very young age and change only when they come up against direct opposition (which, for a variety of reasons, seldom happens).

When an opinion or belief directly contradicts her own, however, a confident person does not feel the need to force her ideas on others — she seeks only to understand where the other person is coming from so that she might understand how the world looks from their perspective.

Grasping that there are as many perspectives as there are people is key to being a more confident person, because it keeps you from having to defend your position from onslaught all day, every day. Knowing that there are facts, and that there is 'being right' (and knowing these are two very different things) allows you to maintain your own beliefs based on the best information you have without needing to convert everyone you meet to your way of thinking. After all, they're basing their beliefs on the best information available to them, their personal history, and experiences. The same as you.

Confidence means never needing to prove yourself to anyone but yourself, because you hold yourself to higher standards than anyone else ever could. You want so much out of life. You know you can achieve great things. But you also know comparing your own exploits to those of your peers is not the way to make that happen. Far better to be a little bit better every day, a little stronger and wiser, healthier and happier.

The results will speak to the quality of your approach, even if you take flak for it along the way.

Confidence is enjoying what you have, but always striving for more.

While you're improving yourself, you should also be sure to enjoy who you are now, and what you've already managed to accomplish. Because you know what? Life isn't easy, and you've done okay. Wherever you happen to be now, whatever stage you happen to be at along the path toward a more ideal lifestyle, you'll get there. For now you're an excellent example of yourself.

Own your uniqueness. Enjoy it. Be the best you possible, and continue to do so every step of the way.

Confidence is not gained by winning, nor is it lost by losing.

'Winning' is a word that has a slightly different meaning for truly confident people. Rather than it being a declaration of their superiority over others, it's an acknowledgment that they've worked hard and improved upon a skill they've been cultivating. It means they're better at something than they used to be, and the only comparison drawn is between their present self and how they were before victory.

In this way, every race is against oneself. Every exam, challenge faced, and successful sale is an indication of personal growth, not one's place in society. To pursue greatness over others is an excellent way to fall behind. As a metric for measuring your growth, comparing your inside to someone else's outside is a recipe for self-doubt or overconfidence.

On that same note, confidence sticks around even when its bearer loses.

For a confident person, a loss isn't an absolute stamp of self-worth. It's a game in which you're able to see how much you've grown in one particular way. If you didn't win out of everyone, so what? Did you do better than you did the last time? If not, how can you do better next time?

Rather than getting down about a perceived failure, being confident means you'll take what you can from the experience and turn it into an asset. To do otherwise is to court failure.

Confidence is succeeding by your own standards, while respecting others' right to do the same.

No two people are the same, and as such, no two

people have the same standards of success.

One person may use money as a point system for determining how well he's doing, while another may use accumulations of free time as his gauge. Neither person is right or wrong; they just have different priorities. A confident person feels no need to inflict his standards upon others. It's enough that he knows what he values and how to measure his own pursuit of happiness.

He also keeps track of what others use so he can pick up other measuring systems along the way. If someone else's metric works better than his, it can be adopted outright, or integrated into his own.

Confidence is worth having, but requires constant maintenance.

It's not an easy task to become a confident person, and you can't simply declare that you are now confident and start to feel all of the things I've outlined above.

You can, however, focus on being a more confident person, and acknowledge when you feel yourself being drawn into feelings or actions that don't sync with that goal. There are few people in the world who are simply confident and never feel any flutter of doubt or self-consciousness, and assuming that we can all be like that is a fool's errand.

By knowing what confidence is and isn't, however, we can all be a little bit more confident each and every day, and benefit from it directly.

Confidence is a good start to a good life. Once you have it, you're far more capable of following any path you choose to walk.

6. CAMPSITE RULE

I'M A BIG FAN OF an advice-columnist named Dan Savage.

If you haven't read his work before, you might want to make sure there aren't any kids in the room while you do (definitely NSFW — not safe for work — most of the time). He doles out a lot of sex and relationship advice, and some of it is fairly off the wall.

That being said, his advice is usually quite sound, and he came up with a guideline called the 'Campsite Rule' to help people who are wrestling with issues related to dating below their age bracket.

The Campsite Rule, in essence, says that you should leave the person you're dating better than you found him or her (it gets its name from the idea that you should clean up after yourself when you leave a campsite). This is especially important when dating someone who is younger than you, but it also applies to the other people in your life, and to life in general.

I like to think about it this way: Would I rather be a force of good in the world, or a negative influence? Would I rather have people happy to see me walking toward them, or running away as I approach? Would I prefer to be seen as a net positive for any project or relationship I'm involved with, or a liability and hindrance?

I think those questions are easy for most people to answer, as they are for me.

But what does it mean to follow the Campsite Rule?

It means that you provide value whenever and however you can.

You needn't sacrifice yourself in order to help others; you just have to improve in such a way that value is produced as a byproduct. You also have to make sure to cause as little harm as possible along the way, otherwise your total impact on the world may be negative.

Think of it like a mathematical equation:

If you do a good deed (teaching someone to fish)

and another good deed (making someone a sandwich), you've got an equation that looks like this:

3 (fishing points!) + 1 (sandwich point!) = 4 (net gain of value in the world)

Four! That's not bad! Way to have a positive impact on the world!

On the other hand, if you're doing good things (curing cancer) and bad things (setting fire to orphanages), your equation might look more like this:

104 (curing cancer!) − 106 (setting fire to orphanages!) = −2 (net loss of value in the world)

Negative two! Not good. Not good at all. You did a lot of good, which is great, but you negated that goodwill by being a horrible orphanage-burner.

Obviously, these deeds and figures have been chosen somewhat arbitrarily, and the equations will look different for each person who does the math. But the reason I'm using math to describe this concept in the first place is to illustrate just how quickly your negative impact can turn good should you reduce your value-destruction, even if you don't increase your value-production.

Knock out the bad stuff and you're left with a significant figure, and a world that is a little bit better than you found it.

7. PERSONAL RELATIVISM

THE MORE I TRAVEL, THE more I realize that what I know to be 'right' or 'wrong' is completely relative.

That's not to say that I think these concepts are worthless. On the contrary, I think a well-rounded, happy person needs to have a firm grasp on truth, rightness, and wrongness. But I do think it's naïve to live as if our definitions are absolutes.

There are many cultures in which it's common to treat women as second-class citizens.

To me, this is abhorrent — of course women should have the same rights as men. But this is a reflection of my upbringing: growing up in the United States as a white, middle-class male, at the turn of the 21st century, surrounded by positive male and female role models, and with a degree of higher education. My background and experiences tell me that it is wrong to exclude women from enjoying the same rights I have.

That being said, if I were to grow up with different circumstances — say, if I grew up in one of the cultures where it's illegal for a woman to drive or vote or walk outside without a man escorting her — it's very likely I would think that way too. In fact, it's incredibly unlikely that I would think any differently than all my friends and relatives thought.

The reason for this is the flexibility of words like 'right' and 'wrong.' These words have as many definitions as there are people in the world.

For someone with my background, 'right' is equality for everyone. 'Wrong' is people being subjugated and kept from achieving their full potential. To an alternative me (a me who grew up in another culture), 'wrong' might mean going against tradition or the word of my religious leader. 'Right' would be adherence to the standards of my elders, or anything that happened to put me at the top of the totem.

Within their own context, each of these versions of me is a 'good person,' so long as my actions reflect my beliefs. There is no absolute 'right' or 'wrong' —

to claim there is would be a logical fallacy. It would mean that everyone throughout history who didn't live according to my modern day standards were bad people. Ancient civilizations were 'bad' for not being democratic, despite democracy not having been invented yet. Everyone who comes from a different background than me? Also wrong.

Looking at it that way, of course it's silly to assume that our right and wrong are the yardsticks by which all others should be judged. Even though it can physically hurt, twisting your brain around to see the world from a different angle is a valuable skill to have. It allows you to gauge others — and yourself — based on relativistic standards, rather than the one-sided, out-of-context ones with which most of us grow up.

Now, I want to be clear: Being relativistic doesn't mean you approve of all the things other people do. Just because it's 'right' to one person that women be treated as second-class citizens doesn't mean it's 'right' to me. It pisses me off just as much as it did before I started any context-incorporating brain-gymnastics, but the best way to help change the world in (what you think of as) a positive way is by example. Exemplify the 'right' you want to see, and allow others to follow. Expecting others to live according to your standards can be just as wrong as the 'wrong' things they do.

The difference between absolute 'right' and relative 'right' is that the former says there is one 'right' and one 'wrong' in the world, while the latter says that you and I can understand 'right' and 'wrong' to be different things and both be correct.

We may use this knowledge to try and convince others of our views, or we may just do our best to live by example (which can make a far stronger argument). Either way, maintaining a sense of relativism allows us to look at people who believe differently than we do and understand that they are not inherently enemies because of it; they're people just like us. People who were raised by different parents, with different spiritual beliefs, eating different foods, speaking different languages, and believing in different versions of 'right' and 'wrong.'

That means there's a bridge. There's something connecting all of us, and it's that — with very few exceptions — none of us wakes up in the morning thinking, 'Today, I'm going to be a real asshole.'

The key is to understand your own perspective while also looking at the world from angles different than yours. To get the most out of life, and to make sure you're walking the right path, view the world from as many different directions as possible. Some perspectives will be close to your own — just a slight shift in whatever direction — and some will be radically different.

Whatever the case may be, allow yourself to know about and understand other views — adopt aspects of them into your own, if they really make sense to you — and be willing to share what you see with others who want to listen, without forcing it on them if they don't. This is the best way to make sure you're always moving in a positive direction while helping others (who want the help) to do the same.

8. TETRIS THEORY

TETRIS IS A GREAT GAME. A really great game.

Not only is there evidence that it can help those who play it deal with post-traumatic stress disorder, but it's also an excellent metaphor for life. Well, the proper way of playing it is, at least.

Expert Tetris players all agree the game's mechanics are simple, but mastery is incredibly difficult to achieve. Without instruction, most people can pick up the game within a few seconds, with a middling level of control arriving a few minutes later. From there, it takes thousands of hours to get any better — all you can do is practice, practice, practice.

The most effective way to get better at Tetris is to spend most of your time on the brink of losing. You stack the blocks randomly, piling them high so that you're forced to think fast, act faster, and decide on impromptu strategies in the blink of an eye. When there are only a few lines at the top in which to maneuver, the entire game takes on a frantic pace, and it's in that most precarious of positions that skills are developed quickly.

The same is true in life.

You get better at life — get more out of it and move closer to achieving your ideal lifestyle — just by living. Just by playing the game and getting up in the morning, you're slowly building up the skill sets that will help you move ever closer toward that golden dream at the end of the tunnel.

But if you're willing to live on the edge, you'll learn even faster. Every risk taken, every rule broken, every burst of energy you throw toward your goals, they all build up, and they build up fast. The most capable people I know are folks who jump out of bed in the morning and start working hard on the fringes of their lifestyles instead of slipping soundlessly into comfortable habits. They figure that if life is a game, they might as well play it well.

The key is not to stress yourself out or lack comfort — the key is to always be struggling a little bit so that you learn more, and learn faster. It's putting yourself in a position where you might fail, and where you might have to put another quarter in the machine to give it another go. You know full well that you will, and that you'll pile those blocks back up and try again and again. As many times as it takes.

Being capable of that kind of tenacity is rewarding on many levels, but nothing benefits you as much as your overarching ability and your aptitude for life.

A few years ago, I got to a point where playing standard Tetris wasn't challenging enough, so I invented new rules for myself. I could only earn full-Tetris points (those are the four-block ones that give you the maximum number of points-per-line-removed), and if I scored any other kind, it was docked from my score instead.

People who strive to achieve mastery over life do the same thing. The standard game eventually ceases to be a challenge, so they decide they'll cure malaria or invent a new kind of mass transit or build a colony on Mars. That's the kind of thing that awaits those who are willing to put in the time and take the risks associated with becoming a very, very skilled player of life.

I don't know about you, but I'm flying through quarters and can't wait to get there, despite all the

'Game Over' screens that are still between me and mastery.

9. PROVIDE VALUE

WHEN DECIDING HOW TO SPEND your time, you could do worse than producing value for yourself and for others.

If you think of your relationships as an exchange, the why of this becomes apparent pretty quickly. You want to give as much as you receive, and that means the more you have to give, the more you can take without becoming a user of people.

Thankfully, what you provide and what you receive needn't take the same shape. You can trade money for products at the local grocery store, and that's a healthy, balanced relationship. Similarly, you can provide praise and feedback for food from a friend who is going through culinary school, and so long as you want the food and he wants your input, you're both getting what you want and need from the exchange. It's a well-balanced equation.

Unfortunately, too many relationships start to wobble when one person or the other gives less than they get. Romantic bonds especially tend to go this route, because there's so much value (of many different flavors) being given and taken on both sides; it can be hard to keep track of who is getting what, and as a result, who is being used. In some cases, the imbalance is permanent: One person is capable of giving plenty, while the other has nothing to give that their partner needs. Breakups aren't effortless, but sometimes they're the best option when balance can't be achieved.

Knowing this, it should be clear why producing value on a scale — but also in small, specific, very purposeful ways — is the best way to grow your capacity for relationships.

This applies to relationships of all kinds, be they romantic, platonic, or even an author and audience situation. Picture value as a type of currency if that helps make the concept more clear — coins, bills, and other bank notes, all with different relative values depending on where they're spent. If you have a lot of it available, in a lot of denominations, it's far easier to make nice with people with whom you want to have a relationship.

Value production is also an excellent indicator of just how practical a person's skills and talents are. Skills are trained and talents are innate, but both can help you produce more value, so long as you let them. An example of this is a person with a green thumb who cultivates plants for fun. Horticulture as a hobby is great, and it can lead to a lot of personal fulfillment. Making that skill practical would mean adapting it in such a way that others also gain from the same activity — perhaps running a community garden, or teaching others to grow plants correctly, too.

As in that example, the most practical skills continue to be valuable for both the person producing the value and those on the receiving end. Unless you're getting all the value you need from some other activity, there's little point in pursuing endeavors that are beneficial for everyone except you!

It's far more sustainable to make sure that you enjoy it — even for a different reason — as much as or more than everyone else who benefits. To do otherwise would be self-sacrificing, and although there are times when that makes sense, as a general rule it's best to avoid selflessness as it tends to be impractical and unsustainable.

10. SUSTAINABILITY

SUSTAINABILITY IS NOT JUST ABOUT the environment, though that's important, too.

Sustainability is about creating closed loops in everything that we do. Environmentally, this means producing energy from renewable resources, creating less waste, and not destroying non-renewable resources in the process (something we've been pretty terrible at until recent years, but we're getting better).

On a more personal level, this means leading a sustainable lifestyle.

Maxing out your credit card is not sustainable, because you're spending money you don't have, very likely on things you don't need. It's an abuse of resources made available to you, and is the equivalent of blowing up a mountain to get to easy-burning coal instead of taking the time to build solar- and wind-power structures that will provide all the energy you need, eventually.

Monetary sustainability is important because without it, you're forced into situations you'd prefer not to be in. In the credit card example, what's the next logical step if you want to continue living outside the poor house? You get a job that pays you enough to pay off those cards, then get another card. From there, you continue the cycle of maxing out and paying off debt, accumulating stuff, and as you do, the chain that binds you to work and a lifestyle that doesn't make you happy grows thicker and heavier. Winning the lottery is not a viable solution to this kind of problem: the only predictable path out is painful, arduous, and mind-numbing work.

Far better to start clean and aim for sustainability from the get-go. If you do, you may not be able to afford all the fancy new gadgets you want right away, but long-term you'll be far better off. Debt will not accumulate, and wage-slavery — being locked into a cycle where you cannot survive without a regular paycheck — will not set in. You'll be able to make decisions that lead to more happiness, rather than being forced to make decisions that will help you crawl a little closer to the surface.

But how do you live sustainably when it comes to money?

Part of the equation is simply living within your means. If you earn $X per month, don't spend more than $X per month. This is simple math, but many of us seem to believe spending more than $X will somehow work out in our favor.

Spoiler alert: it won't. Spend less than you earn and put away money for a rainy day when you can. Adjust your lifestyle to your earnings, and you needn't worry about basic money matters.

You will want to earn more over time, however, partially because your needs will change (and you'll want to increase your options along the way), and partially because you never know what random expenses will pop up, and you'll want to be prepared for those too.

That means you'll need to create more value over time, and you'll need to find people who can benefit from said value. This, in essence, is how you run a business. Figure out what you can make or do that others are willing to pay for, and give it to them. If you're always on the lookout for such things, and if you build a reputation for dealing fairly with those people on the other side of the exchange, you'll eventually be capable of making a fair living for yourself. Continue living within your ever-expanding means, and you'll be a self-contained cycle of economic sustainability.

To be personally sustainable involves more than just money, however. It also relates to your health, habits, and happiness.

You could have all the money in the world and still be unhealthy or unhappy. You could also have all that money, but have habits that keep you from making good use of it. In order to spend what you have intelligently, but also to enjoy the fruits of your labors (and everything else the world has to offer), it's important that you're capable of standing on your own two feet and determining your next steps.

Without direction, you're a bobber in the water, floating up and down with the current, but not really going anywhere.

With direction, you're a kayak, churning through waves toward whatever you have your heart set on. Being healthy will give you the stamina to keep going when times are tough, being happy will allow you to persevere when things are looking grim, and having a versatile collection of habits will allow you to move ever-forward as efficiently as possible: a little bit closer to your ideal lifestyle every day.

Like the environment and like your money, each one of these things should be self-supporting, and capable of sustaining itself without outside help. You may need to see a doctor on occasion, but eating healthily and exercising will keep you fit and strong most of the time. You may need to talk through difficult situations or productivity dead-ends with someone once in a while, but establishing good habits will allow you to churn past most roadblocks. You may feel down more often than you'd like, but maintaining a steady positive outlook will help you get through the tough times and remember what the sun looks like, despite the doom and gloom.

The planet is made up of a rugged, hearty, productive cycle of tiny processes, and so are you. Keep these processes well-oiled and optimized, and you'll find that very little is out of reach, if you're willing to spend the time and elbow-grease.

11. THE CAKE

THERE ARE MANY WAYS TO label a person.

I'm a white, male, United States citizen, who is left-handed.

I'm also a blue-eyed, non-political, atheist, and I like Doritos.

These labels help define me, but they are not me. They sketch a map to where I can be found, but they are not the 'X' on that map. I am the X. I am me.

Unfortunately, all too often we look at the labels other people wear and assume too much about them. He's from the US, so he probably thinks he's better than me. He's left-handed, so he's probably a daydreaming nitwit. He likes Doritos, so he's probably morbidly obese.

What we neglect to remember is that individual attributes are not the most important aspects of a person. A person is the sum of their actions and thoughts. They are entities independent of their hair color or the candidate they voted for. These are just pieces of an incredibly large puzzle: to pass judgment on the finished image based on how a corner piece looks is ridiculous.

I would go so far as to say that the most important thing about a person — perhaps the only important thing — is that they are a person to begin with. Our shared humanity is something we all have in common, and all of us being human ties us together in a way that nothing else can break, no matter how we try.

And we do try. Very hard. It seems that despite all our massive commonalities, down to the level of DNA and heritage, we focus on the small, silly things; our religious beliefs or politics or what sports team we cheer for dominate our news feed and workplace chats.

We're dismissing the important and focusing on the unimportant. We're looking at slices of cake and deciding they're different foods because of variations in the icing.

It's all icing. All of it. Watch the 'news.'

Everything the talking heads are shouting about is icing. It's sugary and sweet and delicious at first, but if you ingest enough of it, you'll die of heart failure.

It's far better to focus on our shared humanity — the cake. It's far more substantial and has taken far longer to prepare. There's a great yeast metaphor in there somewhere, too, relating to our rising up and such, but I'll spare you.

We're so fixated on the silly icing and sprinkles and decorations we're forgetting that at the core, we're the same species. Our differences pale in significance to our similarities. If we would all step back from our petty rivalries and offenses and remember the cake, I think we'd find ourselves with a lot more time, energy, and resources to spend on the truly important issues of the day: Issues that greatly impact the entire world, and those of us who live, work, play, and die here.

12. LOGOS

IT'S ESTIMATED THAT MOST PEOPLE see tens of thousands of marketing messages a day, and you might see even more than that, depending on where you live in the world.

That's a lot of messages. And most of them are trying to convince you of something.

To add insult to injury, many of these messages don't even seem like marketing. Instead, a product is mentioned in a pop song or displayed in the background on a prime time dramedy.

Perhaps the most cunning of these messages, though, is the apple on your laptop. Or the swoosh on your sneakers. Or the charging bull on your energy drink can.

I say cunning because, in most cases, consumers of the products bearing these logos are more than happy to display them. In fact, they'd feel a little ripped off if they couldn't. The logo stands for something, whether it be quality, edginess, or a certain indefinable cool that you understand, but can't put your finger on.

These associations aren't accidental: There are teams of very intelligent people in charge of building up the reputation of these iconic marks. They make sure their computers are used by the right people, and their energy drinks are chugged by the most influential stars for specific demographics. It's an aspect of branding that is part art and part science, and its most shining success has been making consumers feel that by associating themselves with a certain logo — certain colors, certain words, certain songs, certain tastes, and certain packaging — they are themselves transformed into something more. They believe that some of the quality or edginess or cool displayed in commercials and magazine spreads will somehow rub off on them.

In a way, it does. It's said that you are what you eat, and if you decide that you're a Whole Foods person, for example, chances are you're eating more organic, healthy foods than someone who associates themselves with the McDonald's brand. It's not a given, but the likelihood is higher.

This association is very superficial. The attributes that cause a person to eat healthier are not imbued by a brand; the brand simply brings these attributes to the surface. It's encouraging to feel there are other people like you out there, and you're not just a log floating down a lonesome river: You're part of a movement, something bigger than yourself. This is your grocery store.

The important thing to remember is that you don't need logos to be something. You don't need to wear a swoosh to be better at sports; you just need to practice and feel confident with your development. You don't need to drink from a specific can to be the kind of person who enjoys skydiving and snowboarding. You just have to decide you want to do those things and do them. You don't need to have the right logo on your compostable shopping bag to eat healthier. You just have to decide to eat healthier, and then do it.

Logos are shortcuts. They allow us to jump on board a moving train and enjoy the speed as much as anyone else on board. The trouble is, it can be difficult to get off a moving train, and even more difficult to start walking once you have; traveling on foot just seems too slow by comparison.

Logos are labels. They associate you with a specific set of attributes — a movement, in many cases — and if you were to go logo-less and lose those associations, you might find it difficult to express just who you are.

This is something I encounter all the time, as someone who eschews logos as often as possible. The most significant difference is that no one knows where to place you. If you don't have logos that symbolize your loyalties, associations, and — to a growing degree — economic status, people aren't quite sure where you fit.

The most beneficial part of going label-less is that you're forced to figure out who you are down to the nitty-grittiest detail. Rather than being able to shorthand your personality ('I'm kind of an Oakley guy, and I dig the Giants and NASCAR, but I also have a soft spot for indie rock and classic Zeppelin'), you have to know yourself in the context of yourself. You're not 'the kind of person who likes X,' you're you.

This is a difficult process at first, because early on we learn how to describe ourselves as a collection of overlapping Venn Diagrams; the only uniqueness we can offer up is the complexity of the shape the circles make and which circles we use. Being your own brand

— and building yourself up from scratch — is more like writing a series of short stories about yourself. You're forced to understand who you are in a vacuum, rather than who you are in the context of some soft drink's storyline.

As you go through life, brands and people will try to force you to define yourself in terms that they understand, in their context, as you relate to them and what they think is important. You don't have to tear all the logos off your clothing and gadgets, but be careful that you don't let them define you, and reject those who try and force you to belong to one camp or another.

You are an individual and completely unique — remember that, and aspire to be frustratingly unlabelable.

13. LÍFSPEKI

ONE OF MY FAVORITE THINGS about traveling the world is picking up bits and pieces of different languages. Many of the words are direct translations to what we have in English, but there are some that defy translation, and that represent concepts not easily described within my native tongue.

One such word — my favorite, in fact — is lífspeki.

Lífspeki is Icelandic, and it translates roughly to 'the practical philosophy by which one lives their life.'

Learning about this word was a revelation to me, because it made me realize that in the English language, we can easily describe conceptual ideas — our philosophies are defined as 'sets of views and theories' — but not concrete, actionable ones; not the ones that actually impact our day-to-day lives.

Think about it this way: Many people call themselves something, but fail to actually live up to the lifestyles they promote. They'll do this with religious beliefs, for example, or with titles they picked up in Philosophy 101 ('I'm an Existentialist today!'). This isn't always the case, of course, but it's true far more often than most of us would like to admit.

Having a philosophy simply means that you agree with something someone said and labeled. Developing your own philosophy means that you agree with something in a nebulous way, and think it might be a good set of standards to live by — after you've made your own modifications.

Lífspeki takes things a step further and declares that these are the concepts and ideas by which you live your life. It doesn't matter what you say you are: what you are is the sum of your actions, and these actions added up equal your lífspeki.

There's power in this small change from theory to practice. Imagine if all religious leaders and politicians had to live up to their own philosophies and politics. Considering some of their track records, I doubt they'd be able to. Most prominent philosophies are far too impractical to survive real life. They're really nice thoughts, and might even lead to a wonderful world if everyone fell into step with them, but without fail they're too idealistic to be more than interesting extremes — worthy of framing but unable to survive handling. Like a precious antique or one of Da Vinci's flying machines.

Thankfully, we don't have to wait for 'leaders' to tell us it's okay to live in reality.

A non-concrete philosophy isn't wrong, it's just impractical. If you want to truly align with your beliefs — to walk a path that you can be proud to blaze or follow — focus on developing a well-honed lifspeki.

The first step is looking at your beliefs and standards and asking yourself these questions:

Am I living this? Or just telling myself I am?

If the answer to the first question is 'no,' develop a philosophy you can say 'yes' to. Then act accordingly.

ACKNOWLEDGMENTS

I was fortunate to have this book pass through the loving and brutal hands of many fine readers and editors whose feedback helped it evolve from a scribbled rant into a finished product.

At one point during this process, I said the following: a good editor makes you feel like you've been beaten with a hammer, only to realize afterward you look better with bruises and fewer teeth.

A great big thanks to the folks who helped me whip this book into suitable shape for publication, hammer-injuries and all:

Joshua Fields Millburn, Ryan Nicodemus, CJ Richey, Madeleine Richey, Samuel Engelen, Jade Zoghbi, Tahlia Meredith, Mariano Miguel, Eve Socarras, James Gummer, Kathy Gottberg, Alex Alviar, Ian Robinson, Micah Sewell, Erika Donovan, Trisha Suhr, Kyle Oddis, Emily Suhr, Elizabeth Aronoff, Daniella DeLaRue, Chelsea Elwood, Grace Ryan, James Davenport, Kathy Tu, Carly Fuglei, and Emily Tripp.

Any typos or other mistakes are probably the result of me ignoring their damn good advice.

ABOUT THE AUTHOR

COLIN WRIGHT is an author, entrepreneur, and full-time traveler. He was born in 1985 and lives in a new country every four months; the country is voted on by his readers.

More at www.asymmetrical.co/colin

ALSO BY COLIN WRIGHT

Made in the USA
Coppell, TX
12 November 2020

41213975R00049